IS THIS MY HOUSE?

Is This My House?

CHARLAYNE PETERS

Mimmie's books

For
Linnée and Sierra, a walk down memory lane.

Charlie, Louie, Ruthie and Arvie for all the times we played "Is This Our House?" on the way to the pool park.

Fili and any others that come along.
❤️ Mimmie

Here is a house.
Is this my house?

This house has a parking lot in front. My house does not have a parking lot, it has a yard. This is not my house.

Does your house have a yard?

This house has a yard.
Is this my house?

This house has a car port. My house does not have a car port, it has a garage. This is not my house.

Does your house have a garage?

This house has a garage.
Is this my house?

This house has close neighbours and a paved driveway, it is in an urban area. My house is not in an urban area, it is in a rural area.
This is not my house.

Do you live in an urban or rural area?

This house is in a rural area.
Is this my house?

This house is on a hill, it needs a retaining wall. My house does not need a retaining wall, it is on flat land.
This is not my house.

What kind of land is your house on? (Flat or hilly)

This house is on flat land.
Is this my house?

This house has a blue door with a rectangle window. My house does not have a blue door with a rectangle window. My door is brown with a diamond window. This is not my house.

What does the door of your house look like?

This house has a brown door.
Is this my house?

This house has a curved roof called a dome. My house does not have a dome roof, it has a pointed roof called a peaked roof.
This is not my house.

What kind of roof does your house have?

This house has a peaked roof.
Is this my house?

This house is made of bricks. My house is not made of bricks, it is made of logs.
This is not my house.

What is your house made of?

This house is made of logs.
Is this my house?

This house
√ has a yard
√ has a garage
√ is in a rural area
√ is on flat land
√ has a brown door with a diamond window
√ has a peaked roof
√ is made of logs

Yes! This is my house!

What does your house look like?
How is it the same or different from mine?

Does your house
- ○ have a yard
- ○ have a garage
- ○ is it in a rural area
- ○ is it on flat land
- ○ have a brown door with a diamond window
- ○ have a peaked roof
- ○ made of logs

(Insert drawing or picture of your house here)

This is my house! My house has _____

_____.

Acknowledgements

Thank you to all the staff at North Star Elementary School who read and edited this book. Your input and feedback was greatly appreciated.

Huge thank you to my husband, Calvin, for listening, reading, editing, fixing and supporting my writing. I'm so thankful you are with me on the journey.

Photo Credits

House 1: Charlayne Peters, 2022
House 2: Sierra Peters, 2022
House 3 and background: Charlayne Peters, 2022
House 4: Jennifer Olson, 2022
House 5: Tyson Donnlynny, 2022; Brick wall: Charlayne Peters 2022
House 6: Sherry Pryde, 2022
House 7 and background: Charlayne Peters, 2008/2022
House 8: Linnée Peters, 2022

Note to parent and teachers

This book was inspired by a game I played with a family for whom I nannied in the winter of 2021. They lived in a gated community where all the houses were very similar in appearance and style. As we walked by houses in the neighbourhood with the children, I would say, "Is this our house?". The children would respond: "No, that's not our house, that's our neighbour's house.". I would point out a distinguishing feature that was different from their house saying "That house has _____!" (i.e.: a red door, a big garden etc.). They would then repeat the difference "Our house does not have _____." This became a great teaching opportunity. I introduced new vocabulary, encouraged language development, stimulated observational skills and we had a fun way to pass the time. Try it yourself the next time you go on a walk in your neighbourhood or while you drive to a friend or family member's house.

Suggested lesson plan for educators: Create your own "Is This My House?" book by having the students draw and write about their houses. I would love to see these – if you would like to send me a copy of your version of Is This My House, please send it to: mimmiesbooks@gmail.com

Copyright © 2022 by Charlayne Peters

All rights reserved. No part of this book may be reproduced in any manner whatsoever without written permission except in the case of brief quotations embodied in critical articles and reviews.

First Printing, 2022

www.ingramcontent.com/pod-product-compliance
Lightning Source LLC
Chambersburg PA
CBHW061121170426
43209CB00013B/1624